Harnessing Artificial Intelligence for Brick-and-Mortar Businesses

A Practical Guide to Prompts and AI Operations

Dr. Justin Rose and Martin Brossman

DEDICATION

To my family for their unwavering support that inspires me to learn and grow constantly. To the friends and mentors along my journey that supported and guided me to push myself beyond what I thought I could be. And to innovators of all kinds seeking to harness technology ethically for the benefit of society. — J.R.

I want to thank all the people who have been in my AI talks and classes that led me to a deeper understanding of the topic. I also want to thank my stepson, Emery Carr, a brilliant data scientist who is always generous with his time in answering my questions. Finally, I want to express my gratitude and love to my wonderful bride, Barbara Brossman, who inspires me to be a better version of myself each day. — M.B.

FOREWORD

by Dana Gower, MBA CCP ®

Welcome to the future of small business innovation! In a world where technology evolves at lightning speed, business owners like yourself must constantly adapt to stay ahead of the competition. Embracing change and harnessing the power of cutting-edge tools can transform your brick-and-mortar business into a dynamic force in the marketplace. This book, *Harnessing Artificial Intelligence for Brick-and-Mortar Businesses: A Practical Guide to Prompts and AI Operations*, is your gateway to unlocking the potential of Artificial Intelligence (AI) for your enterprise. Whether you're a seasoned business owner or just starting your entrepreneurial journey, this guide will empower you to navigate the AI landscape with confidence and ease. In today's rapidly changing business landscape, it's crucial to recognize the transformative role of AI. Gone are the days when AI was solely the domain of tech giants and futuristic visions. It is now accessible to all, including brick-and-mortar businesses like yours, and holds the key to unlocking unparalleled growth opportunities. Throughout these pages, you will embark on a journey that demystifies the complexities of AI and reveals how this powerful technology can be harnessed to enhance every aspect of your business operations. From streamlining repetitive tasks and optimizing inventory management to personalizing customer experiences and predicting market trends, AI has the potential to revolutionize the way you do business. But harnessing AI doesn't have to be an overwhelming or intimidating process. This book is crafted with small business owners like you in mind, offering practical and easy-to-understand explanations of AI concepts, their applications, and step-by-step guidance to implementing AI operations effectively. You don't need to be a tech guru or have an army of engineers at your disposal.

This book will equip you with the knowledge and tools to make informed decisions and take decisive action. The beauty of AI lies in its adaptability and scalability. Regardless of the industry you operate in — be it retail, hospitality, healthcare, or any other brick-and-mortar business — AI can be tailored to meet your unique needs. This book will help you identify your business's specific pain points and demonstrate how AI can be tailored to solve those challenges, drive efficiency, and elevate your business to new heights.

As you embark on your AI journey, it's essential to approach this transformative technology with a sense of responsibility. The ethical implications of AI are significant, and the authors will address them in this book, ensuring that you integrate AI into your business with transparency, fairness, and respect for your customers and employees. So, dear small business owner, you are invited to dive into the world of AI with an open mind and a visionary spirit. The future awaits, and the opportunities that AI presents are limitless. Let's harness the power of Artificial Intelligence to transform your brick-and-mortar business into a beacon of innovation and success.

PREFACE

> "AI is the new electricity. Just as electricity transformed
> almost everything 100 years ago, today I actually have a
> hard time thinking of an industry that I don't think AI will
> transform in the next several years."
> *Andrew Ng, founder, DeepLearning.AI*

In a time where digital technologies have filtered into nearly every facet of our lives, brick-and-mortar businesses stand at a unique crossroads. The charm of physical spaces, the attraction of face-to-face interactions, and the heritage of traditional commerce have long been their strength. Yet, in today's rapidly evolving landscape, these businesses face a choice: to harmonize the timeless appeal of the physical realm with the unprecedented possibilities presented by Artificial Intelligence (AI).

This book is conceived at this very juncture, providing a compass for brick-and-mortar establishments navigating the transformative waves of AI. But why AI, and why now? The answer lies in AI's unparalleled capacity to resolve complexities, predict trends, personalize experiences, and propel businesses into new horizons of efficiency and innovation. Yet, for many business owners, managers, and enthusiasts, AI remains an ambiguous domain, often seen as the reserve of tech giants and digital-first companies.

Our goal is to demystify AI for the traditional business world, making it accessible, comprehensible, and, most importantly, actionable. From understanding the foundational principles of AI and the art of prompt engineering to exploring real-world applications and ethical considerations, we aim to provide a holistic guide. Whether you're a seasoned business owner looking to infuse AI into your operations or an AI enthusiast keen on understanding its applications in the physical commerce world, this book promises insights and guidance.

Moreover, in the spirit of inclusivity, certain sections have been designed to cater to business owners and anyone intrigued by the art and science of prompt engineering. The beauty of AI lies not just in algorithms and data but in its potential to elevate human experiences, make businesses more responsive, and craft a future where technology and humanity integrate in harmony.

As you embark on this journey through the pages of this book, remember that AI, at its core, is a tool — a powerful one, yes, but its true potential is unlocked when wielded with understanding, purpose, and a touch of imagination.

We are excited to join you on this journey,
Dr. Justin Rose and Martin Brossman

CONTENTS

CHAPTER 1

Unleashing the Potential of AI in Brick-and-Mortar Businesses

Introduction

Artificial Intelligence (AI) has emerged as a game-changer for brick-and-mortar businesses, presenting exciting opportunities to transform their operations and achieve sustainable growth. By harnessing AI technologies, businesses can optimize customer experiences, streamline processes, and make data-driven decisions that drive competitive advantage in the fourth industrial revolution.

> "Prompt engineering allows people to use pre-trained general models to perform specialized tasks that would have previously required training a custom model, possibly at great expense."
>
> *Emery Carr, Senior Data Scientist*

Overview of AI and Its Potential for Brick-and-Mortar Businesses

AI refers to the development of computer systems that can perform tasks that typically require human intelligence, such as understanding natural language, recognizing patterns, and making decisions. The application of AI in brick-and-mortar businesses opens up new possibilities for automation, personalization, and efficiency, enabling them to adapt to evolving customer expectations and market dynamics.

AI has the potential to generate significant value for various industries, including retail and hospitality, by enhancing customer interactions, optimizing supply chain operations, and enabling predictive analytics. By leveraging AI, brick-and-mortar businesses can stay ahead of the competition and deliver exceptional experiences to their customers.

The integration of AI in brick-and-mortar businesses has the potential to revolutionize traditional operations and customer experiences. With AI's ability to understand and process vast amounts of data, businesses can automate routine tasks, such as inventory management and customer support, leading to increased efficiency and cost savings. Furthermore, AI enables personalized recommendations and targeted marketing strategies, allowing businesses to tailor their offerings to individual customer preferences and improve overall customer satisfaction. The predictive analytics capabilities of AI also assist in demand forecasting and inventory optimization, reducing waste and ensuring smooth operations. Ultimately, AI empowers brick-and-mortar businesses to adapt to changing market dynamics, enhance customer interactions, and maintain a competitive edge in the modern business landscape.

Benefits of Integrating AI into Business Operations

The integration of AI into brick-and-mortar businesses offers a wide range of benefits that can directly impact their success and growth:

a) Enhanced Customer Experiences: AI-powered systems can provide personalized recommendations, enable efficient customer support through chatbots, and deliver targeted marketing campaigns, ultimately enhancing customer satisfaction and loyalty.

b) Improved Operational Efficiency: AI-driven automation can streamline various processes, such as inventory management, supply chain optimization, and employee scheduling. This leads to cost savings, reduced human error, and increased productivity.

c) Data-driven Decision Making: AI enables businesses to analyze vast amounts of data in real-time, uncovering valuable insights that drive informed decision-making. From demand forecasting to pricing optimization, AI empowers businesses to make strategic choices based on accurate and actionable information.

The integration of AI into brick-and-mortar businesses holds immense potential for transformative change. By leveraging AI technologies, businesses can create exceptional customer experiences, optimize their operations, and make data-driven decisions that drive success. Embracing AI not only enables businesses to stay competitive in a rapidly evolving market but also empowers them to adapt, innovate, and thrive in the face of new challenges. As AI continues to advance, it will undoubtedly reshape the landscape of brick-and-mortar businesses, unlocking new possibilities and driving growth in the years to come.

Purpose and Scope of the Guide

The purpose of this guide is to show brick-and-mortar businesses how they can use prompt engineering to streamline their business processes and operations without the need for coding or spending countless hours working on tedious tasks. It provides a practical framework for leveraging AI-based tools through natural language prompts to automate tasks, gain data insights, and improve customer experiences.

By following the strategies in this guide, you'll learn how to design effective prompts to simplify everything from inventory management to customer interactions. You'll see real-world examples of how prompts can be integrated into workflows to reduce costs, boost efficiency, and strengthen customer relationships.

Whether you're new to AI or looking to expand its use in your business, this guide will equip you with prompt engineering techniques to implement AI easily. No programming experience is required! Just by constructing the right prompts, you can harness the power of AI to optimize nearly any business process.

Organization of Prompt Examples and Explanations

This guide will include examples of prompts from various facets of a brick-and-mortar or small business with each topic focusing on something that affects the success of the business. Because this guide is directed at beginning to intermediate prompt engineers, there will be explanations of the various prompts that provide insight into the purpose of each prompt. Some of the prompts will focus on clarification of topics, education on topics or business needs, and even providing insight and preparation for conversations with AI specialists or members of a business' Information Technology (IT) colleague or consultant. These prompts are especially useful as they provide clarification on terms and concepts that "non-technical" individuals may not have considered before meeting with specialists. These prompts assist those considered specialists in that the business owner or employee is able to come to a meeting better prepared and with a deeper understanding of the subject. The purpose of this guide is to show the fundamentals and versatility of the formulation and use of prompts for communication with AI-based tools and systems.

CHAPTER 2

FOUNDATIONS OF PROMPT ENGINEERING

Artificial Intelligence holds transformative potential for brick-and-mortar businesses. Yet, the effectiveness of AI is not just about the algorithms and systems in place but also about how we communicate with them. This is where prompt engineering emerges as a pivotal element. By understanding and mastering prompts, businesses can harness the true power of AI. The power of prompts lies in the ability of the user to effectively communicate with the AI tool and produce a desired result.

Definition and Role of Prompts in AI Systems

Fundamentally, a prompt can be described as an instruction or question given to an AI system, guiding it on what action to take or what information to provide. Think of prompts as the bridge between human language and machine understanding. When we query a voice assistant, for example, our question is essentially a prompt. The AI's response is shaped by how well it interprets this prompt. For brick-and-mortar businesses, effective prompts can be the difference between AI systems providing generic responses or delivering nuanced, actionable insights specific to the business's needs. This spans from prompts that are essentially brainstorming to well-crafted and detailed prompts formulated with a specific purpose.

Importance of Effective Prompt Design

Formulating an effective prompt is both an art and a science. An unclear or overly broad prompt might yield responses that are irrelevant or too general. On the other hand, a well-crafted prompt can extract precise information, making AI tools significantly more valuable. For a retail business, for instance, the difference between asking an AI for "popular products" and "top-selling accessories in the last quarter for men aged 25-35" can impact inventory decisions, marketing strategies, and sales projections. The latter prompt provides specificity, guiding the AI to a more actionable insight.

Advancements in Natural Language Processing

Underlying the function of prompts is a field of AI known as Natural Language Processing (NLP). NLP concerns itself with the interaction between computers and human language. Advancements in this domain have been instrumental in enabling AI systems to understand and generate human-like speech and text. For small businesses, this means AI can now understand complex queries, decipher context, and even gauge sentiment. For instance, a local or online bookstore could use NLP to analyze customer reviews and understand prevailing sentiments about a particular author or genre.

The information in this chapter has laid the groundwork for a deeper dive into prompt engineering. The foundation set here primes you for the more intricate applications and strategies detailed in the subsequent sections of the book.

Shifting from Rule-Based Systems to Dynamic AI Prompts

Early computational systems operated primarily on predefined rules that were rigid and performed actions based on specific instructions, while lacking the ability to adapt or learn. They were effective for certain tasks, but their limitations became evident as the needs for more complex computational ability grew. The dynamic Ai prompt system differs from rule-based systems because it is able to interpret, generate, and act on prompts in a fluid manner. This dynamic nature allows businesses to interact with AI in a more natural way that allows users to formulate prompts that provide the desired results and insights. As more data becomes available and AI systems improve, these prompts can be refined for better outcomes.

CHAPTER 3

LAYING THE GROUNDWORK FOR AI

While the allure of AI-driven decision-making is undeniably enticing, it's imperative to approach its integration with a solid foundation. Before venturing into specific prompts and advanced applications, businesses must establish a solid groundwork. This chapter guides you through the initial, yet crucial, steps of laying the groundwork for AI in your brick-and-mortar business.

Identifying Key Business Objectives

Before integrating any technological solution, it's essential to have a clear understanding of what you hope to achieve. Start by analyzing your current business challenges. Are stockouts a frequent issue? Is customer engagement dwindling? By identifying these pain points, businesses can craft clear and measurable objectives for AI implementation. For instance, *"Increase inventory accuracy by 20% in the next quarter"* provides a tangible goal that AI can assist in achieving.

Aligning AI Goals with Overall Business Strategy

AI should not exist in a vacuum within your business. Instead, it should seamlessly weave into your broader business strategy. If your overarching business goal is to improve customer loyalty, your AI objectives might revolve around enhancing personalized customer experiences or predicting product trends that cater to your target demographic. By ensuring alignment, businesses can guarantee that AI isn't just a flashy tool but a strategic ally in realizing long-term objectives. These tools should enhance current processes and productivity while reducing tedious tasks to provide more time for effective employees.

Understanding AI's Limitations and Scope

It is true that AI offers many advantages for businesses, especially small businesses. However, it is important for business owners to recognize that it also has limitations as they are systems that are data-driven. These systems generate outputs that are based on patterns that they have been trained on and learned from vast datasets. Though they communicate in a way that is comfortable and understandable to us, they do not have the capacity to "understand" or "think" as humans do. The ability to match patterns that are comfortable to humans makes it easy to feel as though we are interacting with another human at times. Because of this, we have the tendency to personify AI.

The effectiveness of an AI is based on the quality and quantity of the data that it is trained on. If the data is biased or flawed, those biases or flaws can translate to the output. Users need to be mindful of this fact and that data contains flaws and biases, therefore, they need to be thorough in their vetting of the data produced by these systems. A well-implemented AI can make a huge impact on a small business, but it is not a genie that grants wishes. It is something that requires mindfulness, vetting, and monitoring when used.

Building a Prompt Collection

With objectives and alignment in place, businesses can begin building a collection of prompts tailored to their needs. These prompts act as the interface between your business challenges and the AI's capabilities. Remember, specificity is key. Instead of a generic *"What should we stock more of?"*, aim for targeted prompts like *"Based on sales data, which products should we prioritize for restocking in the next month?"* This specificity ensures that the AI provides actionable, relevant insights.

Conclusion

Laying a strong foundation is paramount for any successful AI implementation. By understanding business objectives, ensuring alignment with the broader business strategy, and crafting effective prompts, small and brick-and-mortar businesses set themselves up for AI success. These foundational steps, while seemingly simple, are pivotal in ensuring that subsequent AI integrations are not just technologically sound but also strategically astute. Chapter two serves as a bridge, transitioning from understanding the theoretical facets of AI to its practical application. As we progress through the book, the subsequent chapters will delve deeper, ensuring that readers are equipped to harness AI's potential seamlessly and efficiently.

Chapter 4

Common AI Prompts for Brick-and-Mortar Businesses

While the universal principles of prompt engineering can be applied across various industries, brick-and-mortar, and small businesses possess unique challenges and opportunities that make specialized prompts necessary. This chapter delves into common AI prompts tailored using physical retail establishments as an example, offering insights on how to craft them effectively and the potential benefits they bring.

Customer Engagement Prompts

The cornerstone of any successful retail establishment is its customers. AI-driven customer engagement prompts can greatly enhance the in-store experience. Such prompts can guide AI systems to assist with personalized product recommendations based on purchase history, in-stock items, or trending products. For instance, "*Which products have repeat purchasers in the last month?*" can offer insights into customer favorites, aiding in marketing decisions. Beyond product suggestions, engagement prompts can also aid in customer support, providing instant

answers to frequently asked questions or guiding customers to desired sections of the store.

Inventory Management Prompts

Efficient inventory management can drastically improve the bottom
line for brick-and-mortar businesses. AI prompts in this category can
assist in areas ranging from stock optimization to demand prediction.
Questions like "Which products have a restock lead time greater than
two weeks?" can help businesses anticipate and plan for potential
stockouts. Additionally, prompts like "Predict the demand for winter
clothing for the upcoming season based on the last three years'
sales data" can provide valuable foresight, allowing businesses to
adjust their procurement strategies accordingly. Users must always
remember that it is best to be cautious about putting proprietary
information and data into AI tools. The basic understanding is that
if you do not want it shared with a competitor, you may want to
research and verify before submitting it to an AI tool.

Streamlining Supply Chain Operations

A seamless supply chain is integral to ensuring that products are
available when customers want them. AI prompts can offer insights
into optimizing supply chain operations. For example, "Identify potential bottlenecks in our supply chain for the last quarter" can
help businesses pinpoint areas needing improvement. Additionally,
integrating AI prompts with external factors like weather patterns
or regional events can provide advanced warnings about potential
disruptions, allowing businesses to adapt in real-time. The supply
chain is one area where AI tools can be used as educational resources
or advice on various practices utilized around the world in various
industries.

Up to this point, short prompts have been used to illustrate how prompts can be useful to brick-and-mortar and small businesses. Previous sections have mentioned how longer, more descriptive, prompts can provide more detailed information. To gain more specific and detailed information about supply chains in a specific niche, a business owner may use the prompt below.

"Imagine you run a small clothing boutique in a trendy neighborhood. You pride yourself on carrying unique, high-quality items not found in big box stores. Walk me through a typical day managing your supply chain. What steps do you take to identify and purchase new inventory? How do you forecast demand and manage relationships with suppliers? What logistics are involved in receiving and processing shipments? Tell me about any bottlenecks or inefficiencies you face and how you overcome them. Feel free to get creative and elaborate on the daily details of sourcing, stocking, and selling your one-of-a-kind fashions!"

The goal of this prompt is to have an AI chatbot generate an educational description that explains common supply chain functions and challenges for a small retail business. The prompt also provides context about operating a boutique store while providing the AI to create details and solutions to the inquiry. This type of prompt provides small business owners the opportunity to improve their own operations while expanding their knowledge of practices surrounding logistics and supply chain operations. They can further prompt the AI by using phrases such as *"Please expand on this information"* or other variations of the prompt.

Sales Forecasting and Predictive Analysis Prompts in Retail

Sales forecasting in retail is essential to the success of a business because being successful ensures that the correct products are in stock in the right quantities and at the right time. With the right AI tool and effective sales forecasting prompts, businesses can leverage historical data to predict future trends and sales with much higher accuracy. Data such as this can provide better guidance for data-driven decision-making on purchasing decisions, marketing strategies, and inventory management.

Predictive analysis can provide insights into factors including customer behavior, market trends, logistics, and potential operational bottlenecks. Analyzing past data against current market trends, AI can provide data or even assist in providing prompts that can reinforce the outcome that you are working to create. Additional topics that can be pursued in this focus include, but are not limited to, anticipating seasonal demands and purchasing trends both online and for physical locations.

Security and Surveillance Prompts

Brick-and-mortar businesses, with their physical presence, focus on more than just predicting stock and scaling their online presence. They must also focus on security and surveillance of their location. AI security prompts can provide educational resources for owners who may feel overwhelmed with technology and how to select the correct equipment or services to protect their store and assets.

Example prompt:

"Provide a comprehensive guide on safety and security best practices specifically tailored for a brick-and-mortar jewelry store owner, including physical security measures, employee training, and digital security protocols."

This prompt will provide a holistic understanding of safety and security by receiving a guide that would assist them in learning how to protect themselves, their employees, and their customers. The owner could continue to prompt the AI to also provide recommendations on local providers of security services and direct them to websites that will provide further feedback from current and past customers. The owner can use AI tools, via prompts, to perform an analysis of the various companies, their reviews, and a comparison of the costs of services before committing to any one provider.

Conclusion

In the vast realm of AI prompts, those tailored for brick-and-mortar and small businesses play a crucial role in bridging the gap between traditional retail and modern technological advancements. By understanding and effectively leveraging these prompts, businesses can gain a competitive edge, optimize operations, and, most importantly, enhance the overall customer experience. However, the information provided here brings fundamental knowledge to anyone wanting to increase their knowledge of formulating and engineering prompts.

This chapter provides a glimpse into the diverse range of prompts that brick-and-mortar businesses can use. Subsequent chapters will delve deeper into the more detail of each type, offering practical examples and detailed guidance.

CHAPTER 5

REAL WORLD APPLICATIONS OF PROMPT ENGINEERING IN SMALL BUSINESS

As we journey further into the world of AI and its intersection with entrepreneurs, it becomes evident that a one-size-fits-all approach may not always suffice. Different industries have distinct challenges, customer behaviors, and operational nuances. Recognizing these differences is crucial, and crafting industry-specific prompts can help businesses tap into the unparalleled precision and efficiency that AI offers. Entrepreneurs can better understand how they operate in their industry, trends that may be employed by their competitors, and untapped markets that AI can help them enter into.

The Boutique Bookstore

Curating a personalized reading experience can set a bookstore apart. AI prompts can analyze reading patterns, bestsellers, and customer feedback to predict which genres or authors might soon be in demand. Moreover, through sentiment analysis, AI can gauge readers' reactions to new releases, helping stores make informed stocking decisions. Ai can also provide recommendations for creating a space that is welcoming and comfortable to all customers.

Prompt example:

"Imagine you own a charming independent bookstore in a quaint neighborhood. Describe the vibe and layout - are there cozy reading nooks and display tables with staff recommendations? Tell me about your inventory - do you curate local authors or books within certain genres? Walk through a typical day running your shop. What steps do you take to order new releases, host events, and engage customers? Now imagine the busy holiday season. How do you manage increased demand while maintaining your close-knit environment? Share creative marketing ideas, innovations, or partnerships that set your store apart. Vividly describe the sights, sounds, and smells that make your bookstore a treasured community space."

The Organic Grocer

Freshness is paramount. AI prompts can analyze factors like temperature, sales velocity, and seasonal trends to predict the shelf life of perishable items. This ensures waste reduction, cost efficiency, and a consistent promise of freshness to customers.

Prompt example:

"Imagine you own a charming neighborhood grocery that residents treasure. Describe the vintage façade and layout - are there aisles packed with locally sourced goods? Tell me about your most prized sections - specialty items, imported foods, or baked goods. Walk through an average shift - what steps do you take to stock, assist customers, and keep things running smoothly? Now imagine you're preparing for a big football weekend. How do you ensure fan favorites are stocked? Share any creative promotions, partnerships with local suppliers, or community-building initiatives that

make your grocery stand out. Describe the warm, welcoming environment amongst the sights, sounds, and scents of your store."

Coding and Web Design Businesses

For those offering coding or web design services, AI can be a game-changer more than in other specializations. Prompts can be tailored to analyze website traffic, user experience feedback, or even predict upcoming design trends. Moreover, AI can assist in debugging processes, highlighting potential issues based on vast repositories of coding knowledge. Prompt engineering is both helpful and disruptive in this industry as chatbots can be used to review, analyze, and even write code for various uses. For users who are learning to code, prompts can provide explanations and education. Intermediate and advanced users can use prompt engineering to ensure the accuracy of code while using prompts to design more intricate code.

Prompt example:

"Imagine you're a freelance coder and designer who builds websites for small businesses. Describe your workflow for meeting a new client and planning the site. What creative solutions make their site engaging and user-friendly? Walk through coding functionality and designing an attractive, mobile-responsive interface. What languages and tools do you rely on? Now imagine the site launches and gets very popular. The client asks you to quickly scale it to handle more traffic. How do you modify the infrastructure for snappy performance under heavy loads? Share lessons learned from challenges. Describe the rewarding feeling of seeing your client succeed thanks to the site you built."

Writers

AI is not just about numbers and codes; it is about words too. Writers can use AI prompts to gauge the sentiment of their pieces, predict readership trends, or even get suggestions for topics that are currently trending. For writers of fiction, AI can offer stylistic insights, ensuring consistent tone and voice throughout a manuscript.

Prompt example:

"As a writer, imagine using AI not just to analyze numbers, but also words and emotions. You could ask an AI to assess a blog post's sentiment and determine if it strikes the right tone. Or predict which book genres are trending to get inspiration. An AI could scan a manuscript and highlight inconsistencies in the protagonist's voice to smooth out. The possibilities are vast for AI to provide writers with stylistic insights, topical guidance, and readership analytics. With the right prompt, an AI companion could help authors perfect their craft and connect with readers. Describe how you would leverage this technology's potential as a 21st-century writer."

Content Creators

In the vast world of content creation — be it blogs, videos, or podcasts — standing out is crucial. AI prompts can analyze viewer engagement metrics, comments, and shares to offer insights into content preferences. Moreover, AI can predict trending topics, ensuring content creators are always a step ahead in their game. Prompt engineering is especially beneficial to content creators as the tools that can be used to assist in text, image, video, and music generation are all based on formulating effective prompts. One of the best examples of the importance of formulating effective prompts involves image generation where differences in words can mean the difference in minute graphic details. This is especially beneficial when creating content involving training materials or online classes.

Prompt example:

"As an online educator, imagine using AI to enhance your course development on [topic]. What key objectives and topics would you cover? How might an AI analyze student feedback to identify the most engaging teaching methods? Share creative assignments and content ideas to personalize learning. Explain how AI could refine your lessons, flag unclear sections, and ensure a consistent voice. Discuss ethical considerations with student data. Outline plans for updating materials over time as AI identifies trends. Explain how AI could help provide impactful learning while saving you time on tasks."

The Local Diner: Optimizing Menus and Peak Hours

One type of establishment that is found in nearly every community is that of the restaurant that has been a part of the community for many years and understands the customers that it serves. These are often family-owned or have been owned by various owners who invested in the success of the business while maintaining the same brand. All restaurants can benefit from the information output and capabilities of AI tools and prompt engineering. However, integrated restaurants that have an established brand can leverage AI to increase their customer base and success in their market.

AI prompts employed in this market can be used to analyze patterns to determine the peak hours for the diner and the purchasing trends of customers. In addition to the schedule, prompts can be used to create new recipes, reorganize menus, create new specials, enhance marketing campaigns, and even create content and ideas for expanding the business online. A restaurant can even utilize prompt engineering to introduce a catering service in addition to their physical location thereby expanding their reach and building a larger customer base.

Conclusion

Regardless of the industry, the right AI prompt holds the power to elevate a business, offering insights that are both profound and actionable. As we continue our exploration, the following chapters will delve deeper into the intricacies of AI, ensuring every reader, irrespective of their business domain, finds value, guidance, and inspiration.

CHAPTER 6

INTEGRATING AI INTO BUSINESS

Harnessing the capabilities of AI requires more than just theoretical understanding. It involves effectively incorporating AI-driven solutions into everyday business functions. This chapter offers a roadmap for such integration, ensuring businesses can transition smoothly from traditional operations to AI-enhanced workflows. Although AI tools can streamline business processes and improve skills such as coding and writing, it is a tool and must be treated as such. This also includes caution in the data that is submitted to and safeguarding proprietary information.

Defining Prompts for Business Functions

Every function within a brick-and-mortar business, from customer service to inventory management, can potentially benefit from AI integration. The first step is to define specific prompts tailored to each function. Customer service prompts might revolve around frequent customer queries or feedback mechanisms. In contrast, inventory management prompts could be about stock levels, demand forecasting, or supplier interactions. Defining these prompts ensures that AI systems are precisely attuned to the nuances and requirements of each business function.

Training AI Models with Prompt-Response Data

Merely defining prompts is not enough. For AI systems to respond effectively, they must be trained using prompt-response data. This involves feeding the AI system with a series of prompts and their desired responses. Over time, the system learns to recognize patterns and can generate accurate responses even to new, known prompts. For instance, if a bookstore regularly queries its AI system about the popularity of certain genres, the system can eventually predict such preferences without explicit prompting. Some AI systems even deploy predictive writing the more you prompt it as it begins to become familiar with how you develop prompts and formulate your thoughts.

Consider an example: If a shoe store frequently asks, "*Which shoe sizes are most frequently out of stock?*", by training the AI with the relevant response data, it can proactively offer insights on stock levels even before the store poses the question.

Measuring AI Success: Key Performance Indicators (KPIs)

Once AI is implemented into business operations and processes, it is necessary to understand the impact of the tools to understand the Key Performance Indicators (KPIs). These are specific and measurable metrics that businesses use to gauge the success of tools, processes, or strategies. An example of this for the use of AI tools might be analyzing the accuracy of an AI-powered inventory forecasting system or the increase of sales from, or activity to, a website after using AI-driven marketing prompts. Setting clear KPIs provides real progress and goals for their business and the tools they utilize. Regularly monitoring these metrics ensures that the AI tools or use of prompts are delivering the desired results or if the use of the tools needs to be adjusted. Researching AI tools and learning more about both them and how to use them is the first step. After implementing either AI-powered tools or prompts, the true value of them comes from monitoring and adjusting them to meet the needs and goals of the business.

Conclusion

The integration of AI into business functions is a transformative journey. By meticulously defining prompts tailored to specific functions and investing time in training AI models, businesses set the stage for seamless and efficient AI-driven operations. The transition may pose challenges, but the rewards – in terms of efficiency, insights, and enhanced customer experience – are undoubtedly worth the effort.

As we delve deeper into the subsequent chapters, we'll explore further intricacies of AI, ensuring businesses are equipped with the knowledge and tools to harness the full potential of artificial intelligence.

CHAPTER 7

MAXIMIZING AI WITH ETHICAL AND EFFECTIVE PROMPTS

The fusion of AI into business operations is exciting, and teeming with potential. However, with this power comes responsibility. Ensuring the ethical use of AI, particularly in crafting and employing prompts, is paramount not just for the reputation of the business but for the broader societal implications. This chapter delves into how businesses can maximize the potential of AI while maintaining a strong ethical foundation. Aside from ethics, being a subject matter expert in the niche you operate brings comfort to customers which can be strengthened with the use of AI. Use caution when navigating into any market that you are not familiar with while thinking AI alone will allow you to thrive. The confidence gained by customers can be easily lost if they feel that you are relying fully on AI and that you do not understand your customers or market.

Tailoring Prompts to Business Goals

The most effective prompts are those that are finely tuned to the overarching goals of the business. When a prompt aligns with a clear business objective, it not only guarantees a relevant response but also ensures the efficient utilization of AI resources. For instance, a bakery aiming to reduce waste might use prompts like *"Predict the demand for sourdough loaves this weekend based on past sales and local events."* Such a specific, goal-oriented prompt helps the business make data-driven decisions, reducing overproduction and waste. The user can then review the data to determine if it aligns with their experience with similar events and adjust accordingly.

One beneficial use of prompt engineering and the variety of tools that use generative AI is that it can assist anyone in creating and developing their own goals, mission, and vision. Many chatbots currently include the ability to utilize a microphone to "listen" to the user's question or brainstorming. Formulating prompts is not strictly limited to the keyboard, and being able to speak to a generative AI tool opens new avenues to individuals who may be inexperienced in formulating prompts or not comfortable with their knowledge, or use, of computers. Being able to communicate thoughts to a generative AI opens the use of these tools to everyone and provides a way to brainstorm or organize thoughts in ways that may be beyond the experience of the user.

Example prompt:

"Over the next few moments, I am going to ramble or speak my thoughts. I want you to take the information provided and organize it as a S.M.A.R.T. goal for my business. When you are done, provide an outline of my thoughts and ways that I can use them to create content or create marketing strategies. Take this information and create a mission statement and vision for my company."

Using prompts in this way provides a starting point for the deeper conversation a user can create to deepen their understanding of their thoughts or an outline that can be strengthened into a foundation for something else. At the same time, it is always recommended that when AI-driven tools are used to create anything beyond personal use, it be disclosed in some way. Although content produced by generative AI is not currently restricted by copyright laws, as of the writing of this book, the ethical practice is to make it known. Just as a carpenter should not claim that a work built using electric-powered tools was carved by hand, the use of AI tools is no different. The majority of the public does not seem to look down on AI-generated or AI-assisted content at this time, however, it is always best to use an ethical approach to things such as while being transparent.

CHAPTER 8

ETHICAL CONSIDERATIONS IN AI

The deployment of AI within brick-and-mortar businesses is not solely a technological or strategic endeavor; it's profoundly ethical. As AI systems increasingly influence business decisions, customer interactions, and operational dynamics, it's vital to address the ethical challenges they present. This chapter sheds light on the ethical facets of AI and offers guidance on how businesses can navigate these complex terrains responsibly.

Addressing Biases and Ensuring Transparency

One of the most discussed ethical challenges in AI is the issue of bias. Since AI models are trained on data, any inherent biases in that data can be learned and amplified by the AI system. For brick-and-mortar businesses, this could manifest in ways like unfairly profiling customers or making biased inventory decisions. It's crucial to regularly audit AI systems, identifying and rectifying any biased behaviors. This is very important as any information created by AI on behalf of a business should be thoroughly vetted, reviewed, and looked at from various angles to ensure that the message is on brand. Any unintentional bias presented in content or marketing can reflect negatively on the brand of the business and be difficult to reverse.

Equally important is transparency. Businesses must be clear about how and when they deploy AI. If a customer interacts with an AI-driven chatbot or kiosk, they should be made aware of the non-human nature of their interaction. This ensures trust and sets clear expectations regarding the scope and limitations of AI-driven interactions.

Safeguarding Data Privacy

As AI systems often rely on vast amounts of data for training and decision-making, the question of data privacy becomes paramount. If a business uses customer purchase histories to offer personalized recommendations through AI, it must ensure this data is securely stored, anonymized where necessary, and never misused. Clear communication about data usage policies, along with robust cybersecurity measures, is crucial to maintaining customer trust.

AI's Ethical Ripple Effects

Beyond direct interactions, businesses must consider AI's broader ethical implications. For instance, if an AI system recommends minimizing staff during certain hours based on footfall predictions, it's essential to consider the impact on employee job satisfaction, security, and the overall shopping experience. This is a great example of an area where subject matter experts need to check behind the information produced by AI rather than blindly trusting the data. Unintended hallucinations by AI may provide information that would go against the recommendations of seasoned subject matter experts and could have logistical and financial implications. At the same time, the AI may provide exactly the information that it "feels" was requested by the user that submitted a poorly formulated prompt. These are two examples of why it is a good reason to consider the implications of integrating AI. In no way is this a caution against integrating AI tools into your small or brick-and-mortar business, but it is intended to provide insight into the part of the discussion that the hype typically steers away from.

Ensuring Ethical Use of AI Prompts

The realm of AI ethics is vast, but a foundational aspect, especially for small and brick-and-mortar businesses, is the design and deployment of prompts. It's crucial to avoid prompts that might lead to biases, misinformation, or invasion of privacy. For example, using AI to generate prompts like *"What are common traits of customers who default on payments?"* could inadvertently introduce or reinforce harmful stereotypes. Additionally, businesses should be transparent about their use of AI, ensuring customers are aware when they're interacting with an AI system. Transparency builds trust, and prompts can be crafted to ensure AI interactions begin with a clear acknowledgment of their nature. As the discussion on this topic grows, regulating bodies both in government and industry are working to get ahead of it.

Understanding AI's Black Box: Interpretability and Explainability

AI systems can operate in complex and hazy ways leading to what experts call a "black box" effect where their internal logic is not easily understood. This lack of explainability raises critical concerns with many as they are uneasy with not being able to clearly understand how an AI arrived at a decision or recommendation. Because of this, it is difficult to audit for issues like bias and determine if the system is behaving ethically. Businesses must prioritize transparency and work to make any AI systems they utilize as interpretable and explainable as possible.

The Importance of Public Perception and Trust in AI Use

For AI to be successfully adopted, the public and users must have an accurate understanding of its capabilities and limitations while verifying the reliability and accuracy of the output. AI is often misunderstood, distrusted, or even feared because of stereotypes resulting from science fiction or even personal biases. Businesses that use AI are responsible for the ethical use of AI while addressing the perceptions through education and honesty about what AI can and cannot do.

Being transparent about the use and capabilities of AI in your business invites two-way communication about how AI is being ethically deployed for the purpose of changing public opinion. By prioritizing public perception and building trust, businesses can create positive relationships with their customers and followers while working to shape public opinion of the place of AI in daily operations and the public space rather than through forced adoption. This is important as many call for a halt concerning further development of AI and more involved regulation.

European and American Regulations Surrounding Ethics in AI

Europe, led by the European Union, has been at the forefront of establishing comprehensive AI ethics regulations. The European Commission's "Ethics Guidelines for Trustworthy AI" emphasizes principles like transparency, fairness, accountability, and privacy. It strives to ensure that AI respects fundamental rights, is technically robust, and remains under human oversight. The General Data Protection Regulation (GDPR) also plays a pivotal role, granting individuals rights over their data and imposing strict rules on data processing.

In contrast, the United States has taken a more laissez-faire approach, with regulations being sector-specific rather than overarching. However, entities like the National Institute of Standards and Technology (NIST) have initiated efforts to create a framework for trustworthy AI, focusing on principles similar to those of the EU. Additionally, individual states, like California with its California Consumer Privacy Act (CCPA), have made strides in AI ethics, particularly in data privacy. While both regions acknowledge the significance of AI ethics, their regulatory approaches reflect distinct cultural and political philosophies.

Conclusion

The ethical dimensions of AI are vast and multi-layered. However, by approaching AI with a strong ethical foundation, businesses can ensure they harness its capabilities responsibly, maximizing benefits for themselves, their customers, and society at large. The journey with AI is not just about harnessing technological prowess but also about understanding its broader implications. This is why many leaders in the AI industry warn against letting AI grow too quickly and want to slow it down or pause it altogether until more comprehensive safeguards and guidelines are put in place.

Harnessing the power of AI through effective prompts is a transformative endeavor, but it should always be approached with a lens of ethics. By tailoring prompts to clear business goals and being ever-vigilant of ethical considerations, businesses can ensure they're utilizing AI in a manner that benefits not just their bottom line but society at large. As the book progresses, subsequent chapters will delve into more intricate aspects of AI, ensuring that businesses are well-prepared to navigate the complexities of this rapidly evolving landscape with clarity and integrity.

CHAPTER 9

PREPARING STAFF FOR AI TRANSFORMATION

The integration of AI into brick-and-mortar business operations has far-reaching impacts, not just on systems and workflows, but more profoundly, on the people that make the business thrive. As AI becomes an integral part of the business landscape, it's crucial to ensure that staff at all levels are equipped, informed, and empowered to work alongside these advanced systems. This chapter delves into the strategies and considerations to facilitate a smooth transition for employees in this AI-augmented environment.

Training: Building Confidence and Competence

The introduction of AI systems can be daunting for staff, especially if they're unfamiliar with the technology. Comprehensive training programs can bridge this gap, ensuring employees understand the AI tools at their disposal, the rationale behind their implementation, and most importantly, how to use them effectively. Such training isn't just about technical know-how; it's about instilling confidence in employees, allowing them to harness AI as an ally rather than perceive it as a challenge.

Communicating the Benefits of AI

Understanding breeds acceptance. It's crucial to communicate to staff why AI is being integrated and how it can be beneficial for both the business and their individual roles. By showcasing the advantages — be it streamlined workflows, reduced manual tasks, or enhanced customer engagement — employees can view AI as a positive force, aiding them in their daily tasks and empowering them to deliver better results.

Ongoing Support: A Continuous Learning Journey

AI, by nature, is evolving. As systems update, learn and grow, it's essential to ensure that staff are kept in the loop. Ongoing support mechanisms, like help desks, tutorials, or regular training sessions, ensure that employees have resources to turn to, be it for troubleshooting, understanding new features, or simply refining their AI-related skills.

Role Transition and Upskilling Opportunities

As much as AI will inevitably reshape the way business is completed and disrupt many industries, it will also reshape roles and responsibilities. Tedious, repetitive, tasks will eventually be automated as much as possible without human assistance which will free up employees to focus on higher-value work that needs human interaction. This will include customer and employee relationships, overseeing complex decisions, and identifying strategic and innovative opportunities.

Businesses should support training aimed at integrating AI and automation to help staff develop an understanding of AI systems and the strategic mindset that will help them be successful in integrating AI into their workflow. Upskilling the current workforce into roles including AI trainers, system monitors, data analysts, and operations or workflow managers provides the opportunity for employees to gain valuable new skills that will transition into the new workforce. Integrating AI in this way enables employee growth that can transform both the workforce and more.

Conclusion

AI's integration into brick-and-mortar businesses isn't just a technological shift; it's a cultural one. Preparing staff for this transformation ensures that the journey is collaborative, with technology and human capital working in harmony. By investing in training, transparent communication, and ongoing support, businesses can ensure that their AI journey is inclusive, empowering, and geared for collective success. The upcoming chapters will further explore the vast landscape of AI, ensuring businesses are comprehensively prepared to navigate the intricate nuances of this transformative era.

CHAPTER 10

Amplifying Business Processes with Effective AI Prompts

For businesses integrating AI tools into their processes, the most important factor is creating effective prompts that steer the AI towards desired outcomes. These prompts are the foundation of actionable insights and enhanced decisions. There are many tools available to users that provide this service, but the most important thing to remember in using any of them is to ensure that you verify the accuracy and validity of information when necessary and consult professionals and subject matter experts before making any large or complex decisions that can impact your business.

Tailoring Prompts to Business Objectives

Users will benefit from routine practice in formulating prompts and reviewing the responses that are provided. This is the best way to quickly develop an understanding of what is successful and continue to develop methods of improving their skills as a prompt engineer. Having an understanding of the internal processes of their business and how the various parts work together are critical to understanding how various AI-based tools can work together in harmony to benefit the operation and growth of the business. Some examples of this awareness include:

1. Identify Business Objectives: Before crafting a prompt, define what you intend to achieve. Are you aiming for improved customer experiences, more robust sales strategies, or operational efficiencies? How would you explain this to a colleague or someone that was hired to help on a seasonal or temporary basis that may not understand the various parts of the business?

2. Align AI Goals with Business Needs: Determine how the AI tool can be directed using prompts to support these business objectives. Understand where the AI's capabilities intersect with your business needs. The option to use prompts to assist in this is also a possibility and may expand your understanding of how to utilize the AI tools or provide new ideas on how to meet business needs that were not originally thought of.

3. Determine Prompt Key Focus Areas: Based on your goals, pinpoint the essential elements that the prompt should emphasize. If customer satisfaction is a priority, prompts should guide the AI to focus on metrics like Net Promoter Score (NPS) or customer feedback. Remember to view the prompts and responses as a conversation with each new prompt clarifying the focus and making the responses more relevant and concise.

4. Craft Quantifiable AI Prompts: Ensure that your prompts direct the AI towards tangible, measurable outcomes. Instead of a vague prompt about improving customer experience, direct the AI to analyze customer satisfaction on a scale from 1 to 10. Use words such as "enhance" or "expand" to further clarify, broaden, narrow, or deepen the information included in the response.

5. Set Prompt Benchmarks: Define success criteria for the AI's response. By setting benchmarks, you provide a standard against which AI outputs can be measured.

6. Regular Feedback Loop: As the AI tool delivers results based on prompts, gather feedback. Understand if the insights provided are in line with business objectives or if the prompts need refining.

7. Iterative Prompt Refinement: Regularly reassess and refine your prompts based on outcomes and feedback. The goal is to continually enhance the effectiveness of prompts to generate better business results.

Continually improving the ability to formulate prompts to direct the AI to the desired content or outcome has many benefits including, but not limited to:

1. Enhanced Decision Making: Directing AI effectively means obtaining sharper insights, which aids in better decision-making. This is especially true in analyzing data or conducting research.

2. Optimized Business Operations: Clear, targeted prompts can guide AI tools to optimize various aspects of business, from inventory management to customer engagement.

3. Improved Customer Experiences: By guiding AI to focus on customer-centric metrics, businesses can ensure a more personalized and satisfying customer experience.

Refining and Iterating Prompts for Continuous Improvement

The formulation of effective prompts serves as the cornerstone for success in working with AI-based tools. Although prompts may seem simple, they serve as the conduit between human creativity and sophisticated AI capabilities. The ability to continuously refine prompts to drive the conversation between human and AI to the desired outcome is essential to mastering prompt engineering and gaining a skill that will place you in a better position for the coming marketplace.

Those who operate a business understand that data analysis and understanding the performance of a company is indispensable. This is just as true when engaging with the AI using prompts and feedback to engage and receive data, providing the user the ability to measure the AI's effectiveness. One interesting aspect of prompt engineering is that a user may not receive the same response twice from more vague prompts, although the output is focused on the same topic. However, the most effective prompts combine all of the necessary factors to narrow down information into nearly the same response at any time. One way to test the effectiveness of prompts is by using A/B testing which compares variations of a prompt to discern which yields the best, and most accurate, results. The effectiveness of the prompt relies on the understanding of the system and the creative thinking of the user.

When testing the effectiveness of prompts and building a collection for your business, a systematic approach involving documentation of effective prompts, their success rate, and providing feedback are best. Doing so provides the user with a discernible pattern while deepening their understanding of how testing and feedback train the system. As these systems progress and become more advanced, prompts will return more powerful and robust responses due to the increase in the data that the systems will be trained on. The continuous refinement and iteration unlocks the potential of both AI and the one using it. This enables businesses to fully harness AI, transforming it from what is seen as a mere computational tool into something that drives growth, efficiency, and enhanced customer service.

CHAPTER 11

THE ROLE OF FEEDBACK IN PROMPT ENGINEERING

Feedback, as it relates to prompt engineering, plays a central role as it shapes the way that AI systems evolve while aligning more closely to both human needs and business objectives. This chapter dives into the importance of feedback in prompt engineering, the method to set up efficient feedback loops, and the collaboration between humans and Ai in refining prompts.

The Importance of Continuous Feedback

AI thrives and operates on data with training data shaping its initial understanding and feedback refining and honing its continuous development and understanding over time. Continuous feedback keeps the AI system aligned with its intended purpose. In small businesses, customer interactions of business processes and dynamics are fluid and feedback ensures that AI remains adaptive. An example would be AI-driven recommendations, utilized by a store, to customers. Consistent and accurate feedback provided on those suggestions, whether accurate or not, is invaluable to the AI output being relevant and valuable. This feedback from both prompt engineers and the customer recalibrate the system while providing input as to customer preferences and trends.

The Role of Feedback in Mitigating AI Bias

One part of feedback that can be easily overlooked in prompt engineering is its role in mitigating inherent biases in AI systems. Despite their computational power, AI models are susceptible to reflecting the biases present in their training data. Feedback provides a corrective lens from the user, showing areas where AI outputs might unintentionally present certain biases through either skewed data or nuances of prompt formulation. An example of this scenario could include an AI system, drawing from training data, presents information with gender or cultural biases. Continuous feedback from a diverse user group can isolate these inaccuracies to a point where they can be corrected. Without continuous feedback, or with the presence of malicious reinforcement, these biases might become more prevalent in the data if not corrected. As part of the ethical use of AI in businesses, this feedback can be used to uphold principles of fairness, inclusivity, and respect to the greater community. Such feedback-driven corrections enhance the trustworthiness of AI systems while providing more accurate and responsible training data.

The Synergy of Feedback and Business Growth

Integrating prompt engineering while being proactive in providing accurate feedback is a strategy for business growth. Businesses throughout history that have quickly adapted to the needs of their customers and market dynamics often outpace their competitors in their given market. Providing feedback thought prompts while requested customers provide feedback to AI tools such as chatbots is important moving forward for businesses that employ these tools. Refining prompts provides the ability to better understand how to communicate with the tools while building a robust library of effective prompts. Customer feedback provides insight into where product recommendation and chatbot responses need to be calibrated to achieve higher conversion rates. Predictive tools that receive feedback allow for more accurate predictions and data analysis that increase the success rate of investments or other data-driven decisions. Feedback acts like a rudder to the AI-powered ship that steer it closer to the shores of a successful outcome.

CHAPTER 12

BUILDING A SUSTAINABLE AI STRATEGY

The modern world seems to move faster for every year that passes, and the introduction of AI has assisted in this through automation and the expansion of organized information directly to the public. This tool also provides small businesses with the ability to take advantage of this tool along with much larger competitors. Beyond the obvious, large-scale, benefits of AI, skills like prompt engineering provide the ability to utilize AI in developing an internal AI strategy both short-term and long-term.

Long-Term Planning with AI

Before a long-term vision can be integrated, entrepreneurs need to understand the core needs of their business. Identifying the needs in the business provides clarity on where Ai could potentially yield substantial impacts and outcomes, whether it involves inventory management, customer interactions, or forecasting. One benefit of AI systems and the tools they power is that they are growing faster than the businesses that will employ them so the resources necessary to grow a business will be available as the business expands. The primary challenges in this growing field includes finding the right type of tool that best fits the needs of the business in the vast array of choices and allocating the necessary resources toward those tools. This is why companies of all levels are beginning to allocate funds toward integrating AI tools into their daily operations. Once these two challenges are met, the primary focuses include integrating the tools seamlessly into business processes and training employees to be effective users of the tools.

Adapting to Technological Advancements

Developing a long-term plan that integrates AI may only take a short time to discuss, but the strategy behind it can be challenging to even seasoned strategic leaders. The AI landscape is experiencing constant change with new advancements emerging on a rapid schedule. Businesses, especially small businesses, must remain agile and diligent in tracking the progress of AI and the various tools powered by it that can benefit them. Just as important in this process is making sure that these tools are efficiently integrated with no, or limited, disruptive overhauls to current processes. Partnering with specialized tech companies or consultants to begin this process can be invaluable and provide ongoing guidance as needed with updates and the emergence of new technologies.

Maintaining and Updating AI Systems

As AI is, itself, a technological tool, it requires ongoing maintenance and regular updates to be effective and operate efficiently. As AI is integrated into business processes, those in leadership must develop processes that determine periodic performance reviews, update procedures, and other internal processes to ensure the proper maintenance of AI systems. This is especially critical for brick-and-mortar businesses where the dynamics of inventory, customer preferences, and market trends can change daily and affect the success of the business. The future appears to be moving in a way where AI systems become an irreplaceable part of business operations with their role as repositories of valuable data requiring more strict security measures to protect personal and proprietary information.

For small businesses, creating a sustainable AI strategy is a necessity to remain relevant in this technological age where AI systems will be integrated into every aspect of business operations the longer we, as a society, use it. Adopting AI-powered tools and relevant skills provide a bright future to small businesses ensuring a foothold in the future marketplace.

CHAPTER 13

CUSTOMER EXPERIENCE AND AI

Technology is deeply intertwined with individual daily experiences which means that AI will have a profound influence on purchasing decisions made by customers. For this reason, businesses need to focus their efforts on prompt engineering and any AI tools that they integrate around attracting and retaining customers toward positive interactions to increase brand loyalty and build a strong customer base.

The Importance of User-Friendly AI Interactions

Understanding user-friendly AI interactions is foundational to pulling the potential of AI that resonates with the user while being easy to understand and use. Despite the sophisticated algorithms and expansive data processing capabilities of AI, its true capabilities are shown when users invest time and effort into understanding how to prompt it and employ the results. The overall goal is not just to have AI and use it effectively, but one that the user finds comfortable and easy to maneuver. This concept of creating a balance where technology meets human needs should be considered if a business aims to integrate chatbots or similar tools into its business model to assist with customer inquiries or assistance.

Gathering Customer Feedback on AI Experiences

One of the most successful ways to gauge if AI tools are effective is by actively gathering customer feedback on their experience with either AI-generated content or AI tools directly. Customers are the end users of whatever strategies or tools are utilized by the businesses that they purchase goods or services from so their feedback on what is successful or not is the most valuable. Customer feedback can be collected using various simple mechanisms including ratings, reviews, and direct surveys. Traditionally, this feedback provides invaluable information pertaining to areas of improvement while providing feedback on where AI is enhancing services or the user experience.

Example of a Successful AI-driven Customer Journey

To bring it all together, we can use an example of what this may look like for a brick-and-mortar business in a hypothetical case study. The Boundless Pages Bookstore is located in the downtown district of a historical town and has always been a local favorite for avid readers. However, as the digital era grew, the store owner knew that the store needed to stay relevant and innovative to appeal to its diverse customer base and be competitive against its bigger competitors. At the same time, they wanted to keep their rich literary and historical tradition with their physical and historical location.

The owner's primary goal was made clear after taking time to think of a long-term strategy for their business which was to enhance customer experience by offering personalized reading recommendations. The beginning step was to integrate prompt engineering to guide the AI by using prompts to sort through vast amounts of data involving genres and authors relating to customer preferences. The owner used prompt engineering to analyze purchase histories to determine what genres customers preferred so that they could recommend new releases or similar works that the customer may like. If the customer did not like the recommendation, the owner would provide feedback to the AI for new recommendations for the customer.

A Review of Broad Applications of Prompt Engineering for Small Businesses

As this guide has explored, prompt engineering unlocks transformative potential for small businesses. Thoughtfully designed prompts help companies serve customers better, streamline operations, and save costs through AI automation. The prompt engineering methodology makes AI more accessible and effective for organizations of all sizes and sectors.

While much of our focus has been on small business use cases, the principles and strategies covered have broad relevance. The same data-driven prompting approach can be applied across contexts, including by administrative leaders. Whether optimizing a retail outlet or managing a global enterprise, prompt engineering taps into AI's capabilities.

For administrators overseeing teams, departments, or organizations, prompts can provide strategic insights, inform policies, and improve performance management. Prompts analyze past data to reveal what works and what doesn't. They can also model future scenarios and test recommendations. For leaders, prompt engineering is a framework for continuous learning and improvement, enabling more informed planning.

Of course, harnessing prompts powerfully also requires giving careful consideration to ethics. Transparent processes, representative data, human oversight, and user feedback help safeguard against potential biases and pitfalls. Ensuring fair and accountable AI is a vital responsibility for administrators.

Mastery of prompt engineering is a universally valuable skill. While this guide focused on small business applications, the principles apply equally to leadership roles. As AI progresses, advantages will accrue to those who can direct these technologies toward their goals through strategic prompting. With the right prompting approach, both businesses and administrations can thrive in our data-rich world.

CHAPTER 14

PROMPT ENGINEERING FOR ADMINISTRATORS

As an administrator overseeing teams, departments, or an entire organization, prompt engineering offers immense potential to improve operations. Thoughtfully designed prompts can help administrate work more efficiently, gather insights, and enhance staff capabilities. This chapter explores prompt engineering applications for key administrative functions.

Strategic Planning Powered by Prompts

Thoughtful prompt engineering fuels data-driven strategic planning and decision-making. Prompts can mine existing data to identify what factors contributed to past wins or setbacks. For example, a prompt like *"Analyze sales data from the last 5 years and highlight patterns that correlate with significant increases or decreases"* can uncover important trends to guide planning.

Prompts also allow leaders to scenario plan by generating evidence-based forecasts. Generative prompts can assemble relevant internal data and external benchmarks to model potential outcomes of strategic options. Rather than relying on instinct, prompts provide leaders a more objective basis for weighing future plans. Project managers can submit scenarios to an LLM with various specific influencing factors as a way to view potential outcomes similar to a wargame.

Enhanced Policy Making

Organizational policies establish the guardrails for operations, making them foundational to success. Here too, prompts can enable leaders to develop sharper policies. Prompts can compare an organization's approaches against best practices, helping identify gaps or outdated methods. Leaders can also use prompts to stress test potential policies before implementation, simulating how new rules could play out across units. This analytical prompting allows leaders to craft optimal policies the first time, rather than reacting after the fact. This can include strengthening policies, integrating examples into existing policies, and using examples of scenarios to create policies for the purpose of providing context or countering any concerns.

Optimized Team Performance

Understanding what drives team performance is crucial for leaders seeking to improve organizational effectiveness. Prompt engineering delivers data-derived insights to optimize team management. Prompts can integrate performance metrics, satisfaction data, turnover rates and other indicators to surface key issues impacting teams. Asking focused questions like "Which workplace changes would increase retention of top engineers?" generates data-backed recommendations. Prompts identifying strengths to leverage and pain points to address allow leaders to enhance team cohesion and productivity.

The common thread across these use cases is utilizing prompts to tap wider knowledge and insights. Whether developing strategy, making policy or managing teams, prompt engineering boosts leaders' decision-making. Organizations that embrace prompts will make choices guided by data, not just intuition. In today's complex operating environment, AI-assisted prompts offer administrators an edge.

Understanding what drives team performance is crucial for leaders seeking to improve organizational effectiveness. Prompt engineering delivers data-derived insights to optimize team management. Prompts can integrate performance metrics, satisfaction data, turnover rates and other indicators to surface key issues impacting teams. Asking focused questions like "Which workplace changes would increase retention of top engineers?" generates data-backed recommendations. Prompts identifying strengths to leverage and pain points to address allow leaders to enhance team cohesion and productivity.

The common thread across these use cases is utilizing prompts to tap wider knowledge and insights. Whether developing strategy, making policy or managing teams, prompt engineering boosts leaders' decision-making. Organizations that embrace prompts will make choices guided by data, not just intuition. In today's complex operating environment, AI-assisted prompts offer administrators an edge.

CHAPTER 15

ETHICAL CONSIDERATIONS FOR ADMINISTRATIVE PROMPTING

The capabilities unlocked by prompt engineering offer administrators impressive new efficiencies. However, actualizing the full potential of this technology relies on diligent ethical oversight. While a previous chapter focused on high-level ethical considerations, here we will explore specific protocols for developing and deploying administrative prompts responsibly.

To start, those engineering prompts must prioritize transparency. Clearly communicate an AI system's abilities, limitations, and training data to all affected stakeholders. This builds understanding and trust that the technology derives insights fairly. Additionally, explain the reasoning behind AI-generated suggestions so end users can critically evaluate the guidance.

Another key ethical imperative is ensuring prompts are crafted using representative datasets. If certain groups are excluded from the training data, prompt results will inevitably be skewed. Continuously review performance across different demographics to catch any biases. Seek diverse input to make datasets and thus recommendations more inclusive.

Perhaps most crucially, human oversight of AI prompts cannot be neglected. Regardless of the sophistication of the programming, administrators must verify results rather than blindly follow prompts. AI should inform human decisions, not wholly replace them. Demand explanations of recommendations to determine if they should be overridden.

Finally, soliciting ongoing user feedback provides invaluable insights for refinement. Listen to any concerns raised by employees or customers impacted by AI prompts. Be prepared to modify algorithms accordingly if issues arise. Keep end users involved in actively improving the technology. By centering these ethical protocols while building administrative AI, leaders can unlock tremendous value. Grounding prompt engineering in fairness and transparency will chart a course to a more enlightened digital future.

Transparent Processes

Ensuring transparency in administrative AI systems is crucial for building trust with stakeholders. Clearly communicate the specific capabilities and limitations of the technology so there are no exaggerated expectations. Provide details on the training data used, including its sources and any gaps. Ongoing transparency allows people to understand how the system operates and have confidence that it reaches conclusions in a fair, unbiased manner. Implement processes for explaining the reasoning behind AI-generated suggestions in plain language. This allows administrators and end users to critically evaluate the logic and override recommendations if necessary. With transparent processes, stakeholders can develop an informed assessment of the technology.

Human Oversight

Even as AI systems become more advanced, human oversight remains essential for ethical deployment. Administrators should use AI prompts to inform decisions rather than wholly replace their own judgment. Insist that recommendations are accompanied by explanations of the reasoning in transparent terms. With this context, administrators can critically evaluate prompts and override any that appear biased or sub-optimal. Establish clear protocols for when human judgment should supersede AI guidance, particularly for high-risk decisions. Set up rigorous monitoring procedures as an additional safeguard. While AI prompts may provide useful insights, administrators must remain accountable for verifying results and intervening when necessary. With conscientious human oversight, the strengths of AI can be harnessed while minimizing risks.

Although the use of AI can streamline processes and reduce the amount of time spent on tedious tasks, it cannot replace human wisdom, experience, and application. For this reason, organizational leaders need to remember that the prompt engineer is what drives the output from the AI-powered tool. Professionals that are skilled in a trade and have a depth of experience in the skillset will be the most effective prompt engineers as they understand the intricacies of their craft. They will be able to draw the full potential of prompts in their respective areas of expertise over someone who may even be more proficient at formulating prompts. Implementing these tools at the hands of subject matter experts is a great example of ensuring human oversight as they can verify or provide feedback on any output resulting from their prompts.

CHAPTER 16

PROMPT ENGINEERING FOR PERSONAL PRODUCTIVITY

While often discussed in a business context, prompt engineering also offers immense potential for personal use. Intentionally designed prompts can help individuals optimize their productivity, expand their knowledge, and pursue self-improvement. With free large language models (LLMs) becoming more accessible, prompt engineering is a skill anyone can leverage. This chapter explores the personal applications of prompts and LLMs.

Streamlining Tasks and Routines

Prompt engineering presents exciting opportunities to automate the mundane logistics of daily life. Asking an AI assistant to generate optimized schedules and task lists can free up significant time and mental bandwidth. LLMs have the capability to analyze your habits, responsibilities, and goals and design prompts that produce personalized productivity recommendations.

For instance, rather than piecing together a to-do list each morning, you could request your AI assistant create one tailored to your priorities for the day ahead. "*Please put together a prioritized task list for today factoring in my deadlines, exercise routine, and need to buy groceries.*" This saves you effort while ensuring you have an efficient plan.

With extensions or connected tools, LLMs can also schedule meetings, appointments, and events automatically based on your availability and preferences. Commands such as "*Book my weekly team meeting for Thursday at 2 pm in my calendar*" handle logistics seamlessly. For more complex scheduling, prompts like "*Generate a weekly calendar that leaves time for my design projects while accommodating my upcoming product demos and dentist appointments*" can yield optimized agendas.

The key benefit is a massive reduction in time spent on planning and coordination. By leveraging the power of AI through well-designed prompts, you can focus energy on higher-level work and personal goals rather than getting lost in mundane details. Prompt engineering applied to productivity and time management minimizes friction and clutter from daily logistics.

Accelerating Research and Learning

For any area of personal interest, prompts enable you to rapidly compile knowledge. Prompts can surface relevant articles, papers, and expert perspectives to deepen your understanding. Prompt sequences can also structure knowledge, guiding you through foundational concepts first before more advanced material. If looking to learn a new skill, ask for prompts explaining key techniques in a step-by-step manner. Over time, reviewing LLM feedback will boost your writing abilities.

Uncovering Personal Insights

LLMs can serve as aids for reflection, meditation, and personal growth. Prompts can mine your journal entries or app data to reveal insights about your habits, mood patterns, and goals. Regular check-in prompts like "*Based on my records, what are my biggest sources of stress this month?*" can increase self-awareness. Prompts can also generate personalized growth plans and self-care recommendations. LLMs that pull from active data sets, or extensions that can pull from the web, can also provide responses to prompts from specific authors or books focused on specific topics relevant to your research.

Getting Feedback on Your Writing

Prompt engineering can help improve your writing skills by providing feedback on drafts. Ask an LLM to critically assess aspects like structure, flow, grammar, and style based on best practices. For example, "*Read this draft blog post and highlight any sections that could be reorganized or tightened up to improve clarity.*" The LLM can also suggest wording tweaks and point out spelling/grammar errors. Over time, reviewing LLM feedback will boost your writing abilities. As you progress through drafts, LLMs can continually provide feedback as you progress. Another prompt that could be beneficial is "*Rewrite the following excerpt as though ready to be published while providing feedback on what could be improved.*" Formulating prompts such as these can continue to improve both your writing and prompt engineering skills.

Building Healthy Habits

We all have habits we aim to cultivate or limit for our well-being. Prompt engineering can help by customizing step-by-step plans to change behaviors. Ask an LLM to create a health habit plan tailored to your situation and preferences. Make sure to frame the prompt with your specific goals and needs. The LLM can integrate elements like gradual goal setting, reminder systems, and positive reinforcement into a personalized plan for establishing healthier patterns.

Mastering New Skills

Gaining both hard and soft skills requires structured, sequential practice. Prompt engineering can generate personalized development plans to guide your upskilling process. Ask an LLM to design a learning curriculum for your target skill covering foundational concepts first, then more advanced techniques. The LLM can include exercises, projects, recommended resources, and milestones based on proven methods. Following this programmed path will accelerate your skill acquisition. Prompts can also be used to pull specific information or provide answers to specific questions about the topic. Keep in mind that you will be wise to verify the information. Some LLMs will provide sources when an answer is given. As you gain experience, you will learn which provide the best results and which tools provide the most accurate sources.

Leveraging Your Unique Voice as a Writer

For writers, prompt engineering provides an opportunity to expedite content creation while still maintaining your unique authorial voice. When using an LLM for writing support, prime it by providing multiple examples of things you have written using your distinctive tone and style. For instance, you can input excerpts from previous articles, stories, or social media posts to familiarize the LLM with your voice.

Then when crafting a prompt requesting the LLM to generate new content, specify that it should follow the tone, sentence structure, and style you have demonstrated in your sample writings. For example: *"Write a 300-word blog post about AI advancements in the style and voice of my previous writings."* This will output new content adhering to your authorial voice versus defaulting to the LLM's cookie-cutter style.

Over time and with feedback on its outputs, the LLM can learn to immerse itself in your perspective and writing quirks. This allows prompt engineering to enhance your productivity as a writer without compromising the uniqueness of your work. Handle with care, but it can be a useful tool among your creative resources.

In each of these applications, the thoughtful prompt design enables you to harness AI for self-improvement. With practice, you can learn to frame prompts that elicit useful insights and guidance from LLMs. Turn prompt engineering into a daily habit to maximize productivity and progress.

Of course, balance is required when applying prompt engineering personally, as with any technology. Avoid over-reliance; LLMs should augment your abilities, not replace diligent thinking. With mindful use, prompt engineering can optimize efficiency, further learning, and reveal self-knowledge, allowing you to get the most out of each day.

CHAPTER 17

HARNESSING THE POWER OF PROMPTS FOR BUSINESS SUCCESS

Through the previous chapters, we have explored the transformative potential of prompt engineering for small and brick-and-mortar enterprises. When thoughtfully implemented, prompts can provide indispensable insights and automation to help local businesses thrive in today's dynamic environment.

This book has aimed to demonstrate the versatility of prompts across critical business functions. Effective prompts distill vast knowledge into concise instructions that allow language models to execute tasks with remarkable speed and sophistication. In sales and marketing, prompts can generate compelling ad copy tailored to customers, identify promising new products, and optimize website conversions. For productivity, prompts can automate administrative work, create task lists, handle scheduling, and more.

Of course, realizing these benefits requires an investment in learning prompt engineering best practices. Thoughtfully structuring prompts, drawing on diverse data, and iteratively refining queries are indispensable skills this book has sought to instill. With experimentation and fine-tuning, any local business can develop prompts that serve their unique needs.

Equally vital is maintaining an ethical, human-centric approach even as AI capabilities expand. The wisdom imparted through prompts should augment human intelligence rather than replace it entirely. Following the protocols around transparency, oversight, and stakeholder input detailed in this book will ensure prompt engineering aligns with business values.

In closing, prompt engineering represents an unparalleled opportunity to equip local enterprises with cutting-edge capabilities. The insights unlocked can help small businesses compete in the digital economy while remaining rooted in their communities. With conscientious application, prompts can open new doors for efficiency, innovation, and human-AI collaboration. This book has endeavored to provide local leaders with the knowledge to craft prompts that usher in a new era of possibilities. The principles contained within these pages aim to help businesses across industries flourish with the power of language AI as a trusted partner.

About the Authors

Dr. Justin Rose

With nearly two decades of experience leading teams across the private and public sectors, Dr. Justin Rose has cultivated expertise across a diverse range of industries from agriculture to automotive service. However, his true passion lies in education and helping others grow. As an educational manager for close to a decade, Justin spearheaded the development of impactful training programs for organizations of all sizes, from local businesses to global enterprises.

In 2022, he brought his wealth of experience to launch Landing Place Solutions, LLC - a new venture focused on empowering individuals, small businesses, colleges, and beyond through productivity practices and internal operational enhancement. With a mission-driven approach, Justin helps clients leverage technology and human capital development to reach their full potential.

Although traveling has taken him far and wide, Justin remains rooted in his Eastern North Carolina home. He cherishes time spent with his family, whether traveling together or enjoying the outdoors. He maintains a growth mindset even in his personal life, constantly learning new skills and expanding his knowledge, especially on cutting-edge technologies. After nearly twenty years spent empowering others, Dr. Rose continues to guide clients to new heights with his latest entrepreneurial endeavor.

Martin Brossman

Martin Brossman is a Success Coach, speaker, trainer, and author who has been mastering the art of networking in the Triangle region of North Carolina since 1982. (www.MartinBrossmanAndAssociates.com)

Martin has founded numerous successful, in-person and online, networking groups facilitating meaningful business connections among members. Martin's computer skills enabled him to create and teach Internet communications, such as blogging, podcasting, video content, and online networking. He has numerous podcast shows and a vast online presence. Find it all at https://linktr.ee/martinbrossman.

Martin Brossman has been helping hundreds of small businesses achieve their goals for decades since he left IBM in 1995. He received the IBM Means Service Award in 11 months, which generally takes 11 years. A real Renaissance man, Martin was awarded "Volunteer of the Year" in September 2000 by former North Carolina governor James B. Hunt for his work with cancer patients.

Even in high school, Martin was awarded a National Science Foundation Scholarship in 1977, which inspired him to write a book on how to make holograms. Those achievements were followed, later that year, by an official appointment as an adjunct instructor at his high school to teach a class on Holography to his peers. It is worth noting that those accomplishments occurred despite a childhood diagnosis of dyslexia and decades of men's work, including being one of the co-founders with Pat Howlett of a Raleigh NC JUNTO men's group led, in 2006, to Martin receiving the Ron Herring Mission of Service Award from the Mankind Project for his contributions in helping men. Also in 2006, he began teaching - Marketing for Small Businesses - in community colleges and towns throughout North Carolina, and he continues to do so.

Since 2007, Martin has hosted numerous podcast shows, including a leading social-selling podcast with his late associate, Greg Hyer. Then, in 2009, Martin pioneered the first social media management certificate program with Anora McGaha and wrote the first book on the topic in NC. Those endeavors eventually led to the creation of a popular course at NC State University called - the Social Media Management and Marketing Certificate Program - which Martin and his associate Karen Tiede have taught for over a decade. Also, in 2009, he received the Ethel N. Fortner Writer Award, which is the highest literary prize from St. Andrews University.

Martin was born and raised in Washington DC and has lived in Raleigh NC since 1983 with his beautiful bride of many years, Barbara Carr Brossman, near his brilliant stepson, Emery Carr. Martin's hobbies include photography, Amateur Radio KI4CFS, hiking, meditation, and competition shooting.

If you visit Shelley Lake Park in Raleigh, you may find Martin riding his bicycle, walking, or taking photographs. If you do, don't hesitate to say, "Hi"!

ACKNOWLEDGMENTS

The forward of this book was written by Dana Gower (MBA, CCP), who is an accomplished business, talent, and wealth strategist/author, a dedicated professional and subject matter expert in personal finance, investments, and human capital issues. He loves bringing advanced education, tools, and techniques to executives, professionals, and business owners in an informative and interesting way. He is co-author of the books *Boomernomics* and *Careering* (both are sold on Amazon).

Dana holds an A.S. in economics and a B.S. in finance from the University of Maine, and an MBA from Rollins College in FL.

Copy editing, book formatting, and cover design were directed by Richard Grassi of Cedar Books (cedarbooks.com/publishing).

APPENDIX A

DISCLAIMER

The prompt examples provided below are intended to demonstrate how AI chatbots may be utilized in a variety of use cases. The prompts could be adapted for use with tools that integrate AI into internal databases or by individuals leveraging large language models. Any text generated by an AI system should be carefully reviewed and edited by a human prior to use. The individual or organization is responsible for ensuring prompts comply with applicable laws and policies.

Salon/Spa Business Prompts

GOAL: Maximize bookings

SAMPLE PROMPT: "Analyze peak times for bookings and suggest optimal promotional hours."

EXPLANATION: Identifies the best times to run promotions.

GOAL: Enhance customer loyalty

SAMPLE PROMPT: "Evaluate the frequency of return customers and recommend a loyalty program structure."

EXPLANATION: Uses data to retain and reward loyal customers.

GOAL: Streamline service menu

SAMPLE PROMPT: "Based on popularity and profitability, suggest the top 5 services to promote."

EXPLANATION: Focuses on promoting high-value services.

Gym/Fitness Center Business Prompts

GOAL: Boost membership

SAMPLE PROMPT: "Review seasonal signup trends and suggest optimal times for membership campaigns."

EXPLANATION: Identifies the best times to acquire new members.

GOAL: Optimize class schedules.

SAMPLE PROMPT: "Analyze attendance rates for different classes. Recommend class timings and frequencies."

EXPLANATION: Aligns classes with popular times and days.

GOAL: Enhance equipment utility.

SAMPLE PROMPT: "Evaluate equipment usage patterns and suggest optimal replacement or upgrades."

EXPLANATION: Ensures most-used equipment is in the best condition.

Hardware Store Business Prompts

GOAL: Manage stock effectively.

SAMPLE PROMPT: "Based on seasonal sales data, forecast which tools and items to stock more of."

EXPLANATION: Ensures popular items are always in stock.

GOAL: Optimize store layout.

SAMPLE PROMPT: "Analyze foot traffic and purchase patterns to recommend a story layout redesign."

EXPLANATION: Makes popular items easily accessible.

GOAL: Strengthen supplier relations.

SAMPLE PROMPT: "Review order delays and quality issues. Rank suppliers for renegotiation."

EXPLANATION: Focuses on improving supplier reliability.

Travel Agency Business Prompts

GOAL: Improve package offerings.

SAMPLE PROMPT: "Based on customer reviews, suggest the top three destinations to add to packages."

EXPLANATION: Keeps travel offerings in line with demand.

GOAL: Boost promotional effectiveness.

SAMPLE PROMPT: "Evaluate conversion rates of marketing campaigns and suggest optimized channels."

EXPLANATION: Focuses marketing spend on high-converting channels.

GOAL: Understand customer preferences.

SAMPLE PROMPT: "Summarize demographics and travel preferences of repeat customers."

EXPLANATION: Tailors travel packages to frequent clientele.

Website Developer Prompts

GOAL: Enhance user experience (UX).

SAMPLE PROMPT: "Review website analytics to identify pages with the highest bounce rates. Recommend UI/US improvements."

EXPLANATION: Targets pages that may be causing user drop-offs.

GOAL: Optimize Load Times

SAMPLE PROMPT: "Analyze server logs and page load times. Suggest optimizations for the top three slowest pages."

EXPLANATION: Ensures faster load times for better user experience.

GOAL: Improve SEO

SAMPLE PROMPT: "Evaluate current search engine ranking and suggest SEO strategies for key pages."

EXPLANATION: Aim to increase website visibility on search engines.

Coder Prompts

GOAL: Debugging

SAMPLE PROMPT: "Review error logs from the past month. Identify and rectify the top three recurring bugs."

EXPLANATION: Targets frequent software issues.

GOAL: Code Optimization

SAMPLE PROMPT: "Analyze runtime and execution logs. Propose optimizations for resource-heavy functions."

EXPLANATION: Ensures efficient code execution.

GOAL: Documentation

SAMPLE PROMPT: "Evaluate existing code comments and documentation. Recommend areas lacking clarity."

EXPLANATION: Aim to improve the understandability of the code for future developers.

Consultant Prompts

GOAL: Client Satisfaction

SAMPLE PROMPT: "Analyze feedback from last quarter's client surveys. Identify key areas of improvement."

EXPLANATION: Aims to improve service delivery and client satisfaction.

GOAL: Market Analysis

SAMPLE PROMPT: "Review market trends from the past year. Recommend potential industries for expansion."

EXPLANATION: Assist in identifying new business opportunities.

GOAL: Operational Efficiency

SAMPLE PROMPT: "Evaluate project timelines and deliverable quality from last year. Suggest process improvements."

EXPLANATION: Streamlines project management for better results.

Curriculum Designer Prompts

GOAL: Student Engagement

SAMPLE PROMPT: "Review feedback from student evaluations. Suggest content areas to make more engaging."

EXPLANATION: Focuses on increasing student interest and participation.

GOAL: Curriculum Relevance

SAMPLE PROMPT: "Analyze recent industry trends. Recommend updates to keep the curriculum current."

EXPLANATION: Ensures that students are learning up-to-date content.

GOAL: Assessment Effectiveness

SAMPLE PROMPT: "Evaluate student performance data. Propose changes to assessment methods or questions."

EXPLANATION: Aims to make assessment more reflective of learning outcomes.

Restaurant Owner Prompts

GOAL: Enhance Menu Offerings

SAMPLE PROMPT: "Review sales data for each dish. Recommend dishes to promote or reconsider."

EXPLANATION: Aims to optimize the menu based on popularity and profitability.

GOAL: Improve Customer Experience

SAMPLE PROMPT: "Analyze customer feedback from reviews. Identify key areas for service improvement."

EXPLANATION: Focuses on meeting and exceeding customer expectations.

GOAL: Operational Efficiency

SAMPLE PROMPT: "Evaluate supply chain and inventory data. Suggest potential areas to cut costs."

EXPLANATION: Targets waste reduction and cost savings.

Administrators Prompts

GOAL: Resource Allocation

SAMPLE PROMPT: "Review budget expenditures for the past year. Recommend areas for cost savings."

EXPLANATION: Aim to optimize spending and manage resources effectively.

GOAL: Staff Productivity

SAMPLE PROMPT: "Analyze monthly staff performance metrics. Identify teams or individuals needing support or training."

EXPLANATION: Focuses on enhancing staff efficiency and addressing performance gaps.

GOAL: Process Streamlining

SAMPLE PROMPT: "Evaluate operational workflows of the past quarter. Suggest areas for process improvement."

EXPLANATION: Aims to make day-to-day operations more efficient.

GOAL: Data Management

SAMPLE PROMPT: "Review data storage and backup practices. Recommend upgrades or changes for data security."

EXPLANATION: Enhances the security and integrity of important data.

GOAL: Facility Management

SAMPLE PROMPT: "Analyze facility usage and maintenance records. Propose optimization for space utilization."

EXPLANATION: Ensures effective use of physical resources and premises.

Managers Prompts

GOAL: Team Development

SAMPLE PROMPT: "Review team skills and training records. Recommend professional development opportunities."

EXPLANATION: Aims to enhance team capabilities and growth.

GOAL: Project Management

SAMPLE PROMPT: "Evaluate project timelines, budgets, and outcomes. Suggest areas for improving project efficiency."

EXPLANATION: Focuses on delivering projects on time and within budget.

SAMPLE PROMPT: "Analyze customer feedback and reviews. Identify recurring issues or praise points."

EXPLANATION: Aims to improve products or services based on customer feedback.

GOAL: Stakeholder Communication

SAMPLE PROMPT: "Review past stakeholder communications. Propose a more effective communication strategy."

EXPLANATION: Enhances relationships and clarity with stakeholders.

GOAL: Strategic Planning

SAMPLE PROMPT: "Evaluate current market trends and organizational strengths. Recommend areas for expansion or focus."

EXPLANATION: Guides the organization's direction and growth strategies.

APPENDIX B

How do AI Text Generators Work (Simplified)?

Artificial intelligence tools that can write sentences are called large language models. They are trained to understand language by reading through millions of books, articles, and websites.

These large language models are kind of like students studying for an English exam. The more they study, the better they get at things such as vocabulary, grammar, and punctuation. They learn what words usually go together to make sensible sentences.

The large language model uses something called a neural network in its "brain". This neural network learns patterns about the English language based on all the texts it has studied.

These patterns help the model predict the next word that should come in a sentence. For example, if the first words are "The cow jumped over..." the model thinks the next most likely word is "the." This is because it learned from its studies that when you say "jumped over" you usually follow it with "the."

After lots of practice, the large language model becomes an expert on how real sentences in English are structured. When you give it a few starting words, it can use that knowledge to guess the best next words that should follow.

The large language model looks closely at the first words you give it. These beginning words are called a "prompt." The prompt gives context so the model knows what kind of sentence you want.

If the prompt asks a question, the model will provide an answer. If the prompt starts a story, the model will continue the story. The model tries its best to generate sentences matching the prompt.

So, in short, large language models learn by studying text examples. Then they use what they learned to generate new sentences based on prompt words. With enough practice, they can become very skilled at writing human-like sentences!

GET IN TOUCH

Want to learn how to apply AI to your business? Contact us for personalized training, one-on-one training, and group training.

Dr. Justin Rose (directly)   Justin@lpsnc.com

Find Justin online at https://dot.cards/dr_justinbrose

Martin Brossman (via his assistant)   Colleen@MartinBrossman.com

Find Martin online at https://linktr.ee/martinbrossman

Our playlist on AI for small businesses

SCAN ME